Oliver's Adventures

by

Brenda Harrison

Illustrated by Dennis Davide

Dedication

This book is dedicated to my little nephew Oliver Goodwin who has brought great joy to our lives.

To all of our Special Needs Children with Down Syndrome who touch lives and hearts.

Print information available on the last page

Rev. date: 01/31/2019

To order additional copies of this book, contact:
Xlibris
1-888-795-4274
www.Xlibris.com
Orders@Xlibris.com

Acknowledgement

I would like to thank my Heavenly Father for giving me the vision and the courage to write this Children's Book.

To my wonderful daughter, Shebreka Harrison, who gave me the encouragement to step outside of the box and pursue my dreams.

Finally, to my writing coach, who prayed for me and believed in my dreams.

Introduction

Sometimes we wonder why God allow things to happen in our life; things we immediately believe are going to hinder us in our lives in some ways. What we don't realize is that God will sometimes bless us with someone or something that is extraordinary.

In 2016 a most extraordinary person entered our lives; the most beautiful baby boy, named Oliver. Oliver was born with Down Syndrome, which is a congenital disorder arising from a chromosome defect, causing intellectual impairment and physical abnormalities.

This is the story of the adventures of Oliver as he experiences the most enlightening things, things that we tend to take for granted sometimes. Follow Oliver on his journey of wonders, adventures and amazing love.

Oliver was born a very special little boy. He touched everyone's heart the day he was born as angels watched over him. Oliver's parents knew that he would have many challenges and adventures as he grew up.

Today Oliver decides to take a stroll during playtime. He is curious to see what the other children are doing. Surrounded by toys, Oliver makes his way over to the other children.

"Hey, how about giving me some of those toys."

Oliver gets his first haircut. His dad takes him to the barbershop. He is so excited to get his haircut.

"Dad, now I look just like you!"

Oliver is so excited to hold his dog Noble. Oliver loves Noble. Dad tells Oliver that it is time for he and Noble to get ready for bed. "Hey Noble, Lets go on a great adventure!"

Look at Oliver and his dad go down the slide! Oliver's dad took him to the park today. "Look at me dad!" "Wow, can I do it again?"

Oliver loves to go down the slide with his sister, Chloe and brother JJ. The Park is his favorite place. "Weee, here we come!"

Oliver stands tall welcoming all of the love and joy into his world. Ready for football and a hug! Goooo Team Ollie! "Look out Dad, here I come!"

Look, Oliver is sitting on the floor at Grandma's house. He is listening to his dad tell a story about the ice cream truck. "Hey Dad, let's go get some ice cream!"

Oliver loves to explore and try new things. Today Oliver tries very hard to get the red pitcher on the table. "Hmmmm, I wonder what Grandma will say if I pour myself a glass of Kool-Aid."

Here comes Oliver! Dad is getting ready to film more of Oliver's adventures. Oliver is ready for more adventures as he follows his dad. "Bye, bye, I will see you guys later!"

Printed in the United States
By Bookmasters